eva
zeisel

COMPACT DESIGN
PORTFOLIO

eva
zeisel

BY   LUCIE YOUNG
EDITED BY   MARISA BARTOLUCCI + RAUL CABRA

CHRONICLE BOOKS
SAN FRANCISCO

Text copyright © 2003
by Lucie Young.

Design by Raul Cabra and Betty Ho
for Cabra Diseño, San Francisco.

Page 96 constitutes a continuation of
the copyright page.

Library of Congress Cataloging-
in-Publication Data available.

ISBN 0-8118-3433-6

Manufactured in China.

Distributed in Canada
by Raincoast Books
9050 Shaughnessy Street
Vancouver, British Columbia V6P 6E5

10 9 8 7 6 5 4 3 2 1

Chronicle Books LLC
85 Second Street
San Francisco, California 94105
www.chroniclebooks.com

COVER: *HALLCRAFT/CENTURY* BOWL, GRAVY
BOWL, AND STACKING PLATES FOR HALL
CHINA, c. 1952

BACK COVER, PAGES 1, AND 3: PITCHER SET
AND SKETCH FOR KISPESTER-GRANIT
PORCELAIN FACTORY, 1983

PAGE 2: PAIR OF MUSEUM PITCHERS FOR
CASTLETON, c. 1942–45

PAGE 6: *HALLCRAFT/TOMORROW'S CLASSIC*
CRUET, SAUCE BOWL, AND LADLE FOR HALL
CHINA, c. 1952

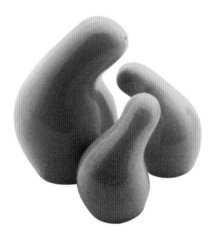

ABOVE: *TOWN AND COUNTRY* SALT-AND-PEPPER
SHAKERS FOR RED WING, 1946

Acknowledgments

Thanks to Eva Zeisel, whose constant encouragement, good humor, and indefatigable curiosity are an inspiration, and to her family, whose unstinting support and generosity have made this project possible. Thanks, too, to Marisa Bartolucci for her clear, incisive editing.

A Playful Search for Beauty   By Lucie Young

Industrial designer Eva Zeisel is a youthful ninety-five and busier than ever. In her lively, overcrowded "tree house studio," as she calls it, dozens of prototypes jockey for attention: martini glass here, three-legged table there, a dinner set that curls elastically up into the air, seemingly defying gravity. "This is a chair that should be better, those are bathroom tiles, and that," she says, pointing at a Japanese tea set, "is a little overpowering I am afraid." She shakes her head as she bustles by, looking like Einstein, a shock of white hair sticking straight up in the air. Her studio, with its colorful stripe-y rugs, tatami mats tacked onto the ceiling, and enormous picture windows overlooking a forest, is perched at the top of a clapboard house in Rockland County, New York. This is where Zeisel has lived and worked for nearly half a century.

Eva Zeisel may be the most charismatic pretender to the title of most important ceramic designer of the twentieth century. Her career spans several continents and more than seventy-five years. She was the first person to design an all-white Modernist dinner service in the United States, a feat celebrated by a one-woman show at the Museum of Modern Art (MoMA), and she was the first to develop an industrial design course to teach ceramics in the United States.

It is one of history's little ironies, however, that Russel Wright, whose career lasted just thirty-nine years and who worked predominantly in the technically less challenging medium of earthenware, is better known by the general public. Donald Albrecht, who co-curated the 2002 show "Russel Wright: Creating American Lifestyle" at New York's Cooper-Hewitt National Design Museum, thinks the reason is simple: "Wright was the greater showman and a tremendous PR man for himself." He thinks Zeisel is the greater designer. "Her shapes are more challenging, her range is greater, she is more of a sculptor. Her forms are consistently striking, whereas by the fifties, Wright's shapes are almost consistently the same."

Albrecht is not alone in his evaluation. **"She is absolutely one of the greats of twentieth-century design," says Christopher Wilk, the curator who helped organize the first American retrospective of Eva Zeisel at the Brooklyn Museum in 1984. "She has a great love of people and how they relate to objects. Her work is about the emotional effect things have on us. It is the most essential and meaningful activity."**

Zeisel's work is now collected on both sides of the Atlantic. Judy Rudoe, a curator of modern applied art at the British Museum in London, has amassed more than seventy of Zeisel's designs. In New York, the Museum of Modern Art's permanent collection contains seventy-five of her pieces (as compared with eighteen of Russel Wright's).

Zeisel's career, like that of many a creative individual, has progressed in fits and starts. In the 1960s she stopped designing. In the 1980s she suddenly started up again, and now at the turn of the twenty-first century she has become the beloved role model for a new generation of American designers. Karim Rashid, whose colorful bloblike furniture, lighting, and tabletop designs have won him international recognition, says: "Her organic sensibility and attention to the communication of beauty has greatly inspired me." He happily recommended her to the tabletop company, Nambé, in Santa Fe, where she has now designed twenty-two items in metal and crystal (platters, vases, wineglasses, and lamps).

Eva Zeisel's life is as extraordinary as her work. She doesn't consciously follow trends, doesn't bow to convention, and has always followed her own path, living life like the heroine of a particularly outlandish historical novel. Driven by curiosity and an overriding passion for new experiences, she crossed continents traveling alone in an era when women were not expected (or even permitted) to go to dinner parties without a chaperone. By age twenty-nine, she was living in communist Russia, where she would wind up in solitary confinement for nearly twelve months. She escaped death by a hair's breadth and says, "Ever since my life has been a gift."

She was born Eva Amalia Striker, on November 13, 1906, into a wealthy, Budapest family. Her father, Alexander Striker, was a prosperous textile factory owner, and her mother, Laura Polanyi Striker, was a feminist, a historian, and the first woman to receive a doctorate at a university in Hungary. She ran a progressive kindergarten where the pupils learned about painting, music, and modern dance. Laura Striker was evidently an eccentric mixture of nineteenth-century morality and bohemian liberalism. Nudity was fine for her three children, but she took her own baths wearing a slip because she thought it unseemly to expose her body even in private.

The young Eva was playful but extremely single-minded. As a child she refused to sleep indoors in summer, preferring to camp out under the blossoming peach, pomegranate, almond, and filbert trees in the family garden with her beloved German shepherd and a ragtag bunch of kittens for company.

At eighteen Zeisel enrolled in the Kepzomuveszeti Academia (the Budapest Royal Academy of Fine Arts) to become a painter. But after eighteen months she quit. Her mother insisted that she learn a skill or trade, so she enrolled as an apprentice with a local potter in a run-down section of the city. She became the first woman member of the Hungarian Guild of Chimney Sweeps, Oven Makers, Roof Tilers, Well Diggers, and Potters. She trod clay with her bare feet, and traveled from house to house with her master, repairing and installing tiled ovens.

Just before her twenty-first birthday, Eva answered an ad in a trade journal and landed her second job, at an art-pottery studio, Hansa Kunstkeramik in Hamburg, Germany. Here she worked in Dickensian squalor above a courtyard full of pigs and rubbish, two blocks from the red-light district. Her colleagues included a gnarled ex-seaman and a deaf-mute hunchback who smelled so bad she doused him with cologne every morning. Charmed by her ministrations, he took it upon himself to protect her. "When we got paid, he invited his friends around, mostly blind beggars, and we all had drinks," she said.

Unfortunately, Zeisel was not able to throw pots with sufficient consistency to copy the shapes sold by the studio. After six months she returned home to Budapest. For a time she designed avant-garde theater sets, but her dream of working as a ceramic designer was not forgotten. In the fall of 1928 she responded to another ad, this time for a job as an industrial designer at the Schramberger Majolika Fabrik (known familiarly as Schramberg) in the Black Forest. One of the top five factories in Germany, it employed nearly 350 people.

Before arriving at Schramberg, Eva immersed herself in the rudiments of drafting to prepare for the task of designing on paper. With her compass and ruler she started out creating what she calls "the most absurd shapes." "They looked like a flat piece when they were put into three dimensions. I was extremely surprised," she says. For a long time she continued with these "absurd" geometric forms because they sold so well.

The Schramberg factory had been renowned for its folk-ornamented designs, but after Eva's arrival the factory began exporting her colorful, geometric shapes—mostly to America. During her time at the factory, she would fashion more than 200 new designs. The city of Schramberg continues to be proud of her contribution. In 2000 it named one of its streets after her.

A major stylistic influence on Zeisel at this time was the Modernist architecture that had begun popping up in magazines like *Die Form*. **"I was fascinated by some beautiful modern villas, which I visited several times. Soon some of my inkwells started to look like tiny modern villas. And when a few years later buildings and cars began to feature rounded corners—my tea sets, ashtrays, and inkwells followed suit."**

She was envious of the students at the Bauhaus because their designs were considered "proper, accepted, and prestigious." However, she was not overly impressed by their ceramics. "Surprisingly," she says, "the Bauhaus did only round pottery things inspired by handicraft."

Zeisel bought her first camera the same year she moved to Schramberg. She was a good photographer and soon convinced the company that she should design their advertisements, too. She wanted her designs to be presented in a new way, using moody shadows to highlight the shapes and show the relationships between different pieces. "I hardly ever photographed one thing alone," she recalls. Before long she was also conceiving exhibition stands and preparing the presentations for the traveling salesmen.

Eventually, the model makers at Schramberg started handing her unfinished plaster and plasticine pieces so she could further form them. **This is how she arrived at her current work process: starting with drawings on paper and paper cutouts, then carving shapes. "I found that the finesse and very much of the details you can't realize on paper."** The softening of her shapes is likely a result of this hands-on approach. "Everything I do is a direct creation of my hands whether it is made in wood, plaster, or clay," Zeisel says of her work. She is no fan of computer-aided design, because it lacks the emotional connection and the tactility of manual modeling. "Computer shapes will always be cold, strange, not beautiful," she insists.

The most elegant time of her life started in the summer of 1930 when Zeisel's mother rented a studio in Berlin for her and her eldest brother, Michael, a patent attorney. The studio was five doors away from the famous Romanisches Café, considered by many progressive intellectuals of the time to be the center of the world. Zeisel's uncle Michael Polanyi, a well-known physicist, and her cousin Anna Seghers, a prominent writer, also lived in Berlin and introduced her to a lively group of intellectuals. "The discussions often went over from the café to my apartment," she says, shutting her eyes tight at this pleasant memory. During this time she encountered two men who would play fateful roles in her life, Alex Weissberg and Hans Zeisel.

By 1931 she was employed by Christian Carstens Kommerz Gesellschaft, a family outfit that ran several factories in Germany. She designed from home in Berlin and occasionally visited the factories to supervise production. This working method became the blueprint for her entire American career.

In Berlin, Russian culture was all the rage. Eva enjoyed the Russian cabaret, concerts by Russian folksingers, and exhibitions of Russian children's books. On a whim, wanting to see this grand social experiment in person, she set off for Russia on January 1, 1932.

Her beau, the physicist Alex Weissberg, was already working at a technical institute in Kharkov and secured a visa for her by saying they were engaged. A matter of days after her arrival, Zeisel visited a local plate factory and the government-run Ukrainian China and Glass Trust. The head of the trust engaged her on the spot and within two weeks packed her off to visit the outlying ceramic factories in the Ukraine. While in the Soviet Union she would marry Weissberg; it was a marriage more of social convenience than romantic commitment.

"Traveling was high comedy," Zeisel says. Once she had to spend a night in a train station and slept in her leather boots and coat on a long table. She awoke the next morning to find breakfast going on around her—literally. At the next town she was obliged to wait for twenty-four hours in the snow for a truck, while, she says, "the tears were streaming down my face." When she finally arrived at the factory she was reprimanded: "What kind of time is this to arrive?" But she found on each pottery wheel a geranium in her honor. "They hardly ever had a visitor and I was considered very official."

"The whole country at that time smelled of old, wet clothes," she says. "It was a time of very great famine. *The Listener,* a magazine in London, said that nobody knows for sure if there was a real famine because no foreigner was there. But I was there. They ate their cats and dogs first and then their in-laws." One police chief tried to impress her by showing her photographs he had taken of "the cannibals."

Within six months, the head of the trust had her transferred to the prestigious Lomonosov Porcelain Factory near St. Petersburg. Founded in 1844 as the Imperial

Porcelain Factory by the daughter of Peter the Great, Lomonosov still had an impressive museum for its ornate designs and departments for making porcelain false teeth, eyes for the blind, and diplomatic gifts. In addition, there was a new experimental department run by the Suprematist artist Nikolai Suetin, who once spent an entire day contemplating the placement of one small red dot on one of Eva's designs.

By the early thirties, the Russians had become very interested in design, Eva recalls. "When I arrived, Lomonosov had no new shapes. They made standard shapes from old molds and ornamented them," she says. She found the Suprematists completely different from Western designers. "They said the simplicity of the West was decadent. They despised the Bauhaus because they said their simplicity was brought about by the downfall of capitalism."

However, Suetin did experiment with new shapes, creating some Cubist-looking forms, and **Zeisel, for her part, continued her own exploration of softer rounded shapes, often in combination with strikingly simple geometric decoration. She was now advancing her skills using porcelain, a particularly treacherous material.** "Earthenware keeps its form, because it isn't fired at very high temperatures, so many shapes can be made easily in earthenware," she explains. "But porcelain gets soft and close to melting when it is fired, so it is much harder to manipulate."

By 1934 she was transferred again, this time to Dulevo, near Moscow, the second-largest ceramic factory in the world (the largest was Homer Loughlin in the United States). Then in 1935, when just twenty-nine years old, she was promoted to artistic director of the China and Glass Industry. Asked how she landed such an important job, Zeisel gives a Garboesque shrug and replies, "Personal charm."

One of her tasks was to create a standardized dinner service for use throughout the country, but as the project neared completion, state directives changed and the scheme was scrapped. However, many of her new ceramics designs were put into production, as were her designs for porcelain electric fixtures, glass bottles for the perfume industry, and store interiors. For one store in Moscow, she was told on no account to include any of those "gynecologist's chairs"—a reference to Le Corbusier's metal-and-leather chaise longue!

Her success brought her enemies, and several months later in May 1936 Zeisel was arrested in Moscow. Her alleged crime was plotting to assassinate Stalin. For sixteen months she was held in various prisons and interrogated; she was kept in solitary confinement for twelve of them.

To stay sane, Zeisel tried to exercise what she calls "thought control": She banned all reminiscences of her past and daydreams of her future. Instead she focused on the here and now with mind games like imagining how she would construct a bra. She kept physically fit by performing rudimentary gymnastics—mostly headstands or bicycling in the air.

Zeisel so efficiently trained herself to live in the moment that sixty years later she remarks: "When someone says let's make a date for Wednesday, it has no reality. Eternity is only in the present, and when the present is filled with disharmony, it is lost."

After ten months in solitary, Zeisel feared that her situation was hopeless. One of her neighbors in prison went mad, screaming and gnawing at her hands, and another tried to hang herself. Then, one night Eva overheard a man being interrogated. He denied knowing Eva but was told, "Your deposition makes no difference, we will destroy her anyway." Despairing and under enormous pressure to implicate others to secure her own freedom, Eva took a piece of copper wire from the toilet tank and tried to slit her wrists. Fortunately, she was saved by her own incompetence.

On September 17, 1937, she was taken out of her cell to what she thought would be her execution. Instead, she was put on a train to Vienna where her Aunt Sophie, her brother Michael, and her friend Hans Zeisel now lived. A fellow passenger, thinking he was flattering Eva, told her she looked "not a day over forty-five." She had just turned thirty.

Six months later Hitler annexed Austria. Unable to stand more emotional stress, Zeisel caught the last train out of the country and escaped to England on her own. Here she recounted her prison experiences to her childhood friend Arthur Koestler, who had himself been a prisoner in a Spanish death cell. That summer he began work on his next novel, *Darkness at Noon,* about the victims of Stalin's purges, basing it on his and Zeisel's experiences. Together they lobbied for the release of Zeisel's mother, whom the Gestapo had arrested in Austria. Her mother was eventually freed, but her aunt, uncle, and many family friends were sent to concentration camps.

Hans Zeisel came to England in the summer of 1938 and the pair married (her "divorce" from Weissberg was arranged before she left Vienna). In October, the newly-weds sailed to New York. They had $64 between them. Eva recalls that the city was swamped with European immigrants. "All sorts of elegant gentlemen were sitting on benches along Broadway: professors, ministers, and members of parliament, very respectable citizens. They sat there not knowing what to do or how to integrate. And their wives, very elegant respectable ladies, earned a little money by cleaning house or working as cooks."

Zeisel was not about to sit down and weep. On her second day in Manhattan, she headed to the public library to look up design magazines. Her plan was to contact editors in hopes of obtaining introductions to manufacturers. She soon hooked up with the Bay Ridge Specialty Company in New Jersey and began designing a line of giftware.

Initially, she took on whatever work was offered. She made a plaster model of the Himalayas for a film company (earning fifty cents an hour) and designed watches, miniature dishes, and china decals. "It was not a question of whether or not I enjoyed the work, but whether I could afford a whole apple pie or half of one," she chuckles.

While modeling the Himalayas, Zeisel met Karl Johnson, a student from the Pratt Institute, and the two set up in business together. They worked out of a room on the Pratt campus in Brooklyn. One day the head of industrial design stopped by for a chat. He was so impressed by Eva, he asked her to develop a course in mass-produced ceramic design that she could teach. Until then ceramics had been taught in American design schools as a handicraft.

Zeisel gave the students tasks like creating forms that communicate such notions as "growing," "cozy," "compact," "cheerful," "melting," "slim," and "crisp," in order to teach them about the expressiveness of line. It was a technique she herself always employed to model shapes. She asked her students to imagine how a handle would feel, how a pot would balance in the hand, how light would affect an object, how the shadowed parts might disappear, altering the apparent dimensions of a shape.

In 1940 Zeisel gave birth to her first child, Jean (her son, John, was born in 1944). Later that year Eliot Noyes, director of the design department at MoMA, paid a visit to her student show. He questioned Zeisel about some square food canisters. "He thought ceramics ought to be round. He came from an Arts and Crafts background," she says wryly. Noyes was nevertheless impressed, and in 1942 he recommended to Castleton China that Zeisel design and create the first all-white china service in the United States. Noyes said the museum would give the line its imprimatur and launch the collection with a special exhibition, so long as it retained the right to approve every piece.

"They were very puritan," Zeisel says of her dealings with the museum. **"At the time they didn't permit decoration and there were certain objects they considered too chichi, so they excluded them."** She was ideologically opposed to the Modern movement that MoMA championed. Her grievance (which she drummed into her students during her fifteen years at Pratt) was that designs should communicate, and with the Modern movement communication was cut off. "For the Moderns, things were not supposed to be soulful friends but mute slaves serving us."

Nevertheless, Zeisel managed to create an impressively sophisticated design for Castleton. She had read Emily Post to learn all about the etiquette of the American table and shaped the service to illustrate the words "dignified," "erect," "uplifted." "I wanted it to look as if it was growing up from the table," she says. Each piece starts out as straight lines that soften into curves. The walls of each design are thickest at the bottom and taper as they rise.

In Europe, Trude Petri's Urbino dinner service for Staatliche Porzellan Manufaktur in Cologne predated the Museum service as the first white dinner service by over a decade. But Petri's work was formally simplistic and rather lumpy in appearance. By contrast, the Museum service was an extraordinary piece of virtuoso design and the first attempt internationally to meld formal dinnerware with the ideals of modernism. "To make china this way is very technically demanding," marvels Christopher Wilk. The design, he continues, is also a delight to use. "It is compulsively tactile."

Because the war halted production of the dinner service, MoMA delayed the exhibition celebrating the Museum line until 1946. When it finally opened, the show attracted national attention and effectively launched Zeisel's American career. "It made me an accepted first-class designer rather than a run-of-the-mill designer," she says. It placed her firmly in the league of such American innovators as Frederick H. Rhead, who created Fiestaware in 1935 (several years after Zeisel developed her own bold geometric pieces for Schramberg in Germany), and Russel Wright, with his revolutionary lifestyle ideas and relaxed, colorful dinnerware.

Initially, Zeisel's business changed little. It was still an uphill struggle. She continued to send out huge volleys of letters to manufacturers asking for work. She was still financially strapped (even though Hans was now teaching economics at Rutgers University) and couldn't afford to buy any of the Museum line for herself. It was a sentiment shared by much of the American public. "One coffeepot was $45!" she says, rolling her eyes. When she visited factories in the Midwest, she drove through the night and didn't stop, to avoid spending money on hotels. Too poor to buy gifts for her two children, she wrote them poems instead. "She would type them up badly and hand them to us," said daughter Jean Richards, now an actress and author.

Among collectors and museum curators, one of Zeisel's most cherished designs is her 1946 Town and Country service for the Minnesota-based manufacturer Red Wing. The company wanted a design that would be young, free-spirited, "Greenwich Village-y," and affordable. Town and Country's capacious, curvaceous, off-kilter shapes epitomize Zeisel's playful spirit and encapsulate her belief that designs should communicate with one another and engage us through their friendly, zoomorphic shapes.

The intimately angled salt-and-pepper shakers of this set are best-sellers and beloved by Zeisel fans. They are based on her favorite design inspiration, mother and child nestling together. Other recurring shapes are belly buttons, breasts, baby bottoms, ripe fruits, and flocks of birds. **On close inspection, many of Zeisel's curvaceous forms appear to reticulate, playing off the positive and negative shapes beside them. "They make love to each other," she laughs.**

The late 1940s was a halcyon period for Zeisel, and commissions flooded in from all over the country. She designed for Sears, Roebuck and Co., Butler Brothers, Charm House, General Mills, Salisbury Artisans, Riverside China, and United China and Glass, among others. She also established her own studio in the basement of her apartment house on New York's Riverside Drive. It was a whitewashed circular space with boldly striped rugs and desks cantilevered from the walls.

Another one of Zeisel's most celebrated and successful designs is Hallcraft/Tomorrow's Classic. It very nearly didn't reach production. The manufacturer, Hall China, was on the point of shelving it when the president of Commercial Decal stepped in saying he thought the pieces were ideal for decoration. Consequently, Eva was required to present nine patterns the first year and three each subsequent year.

Tomorrow's Classic, with its sensuous swelling forms and very affordable price tag (just $8.95 for a sixteen-piece set), was a meteoric success. It grossed $250,000 in twelve months during 1952. Royalty checks poured in for $600 to $700 a month, and with the $1,000 advance money Zeisel purchased a rambling clapboard house, on the same street as John Houseman, Lotte Lenya, and Richard Pousette-Dart, at the foot of South Mountain in Rockland County, New York. It was all a far cry from the Red Wing era when she had foolishly settled for a simple $300 flat fee.

In 1953 Zeisel resigned from Pratt. The University of Chicago had offered her husband a professorship in law and sociology, and the family moved to Illinois. Zeisel could never juggle family and work easily. "I don't know how other women managed it," she sighs. "Hans thought my work should be second to his." In conventional university surroundings, her creative energies wilted. After a year she and the children returned to New York. For the next sixteen years she shuttled back and forth, trying to hold family and work together.

Hall China was so elated by the success of Tomorrow's Classic, it soon commissioned Zeisel to create another exquisitely refined service, the Hallcraft/Century line. Its delicate petal-shaped plates rise up like the graceful arc of a ballerina's arm. While its extravagantly attenuated forms were beautiful to behold, the service was not well suited to packing and shipping. The pieces often broke in transport. Unlike Tomorrow's Classic, Century was not a commercial success.

Around this period Zeisel was courted by the glass industry and worked for three manufacturers, Bryce Brothers, Federal Glass, and Heisey. At Federal Glass her Prestige line was a massive hit. The factory produced a glass a second at the height of the line's success and sold the glass all over the world at the rock-bottom price of twelve cents apiece. Zeisel manipulated the reflections in the base of the glass to create an optical trick. "You think the base is very heavy and solid, but it is actually one-sixteenth of an inch thick in the middle," she says.

By the late 1950s the china industry in the United States was in decline. Steubenville Pottery, which had made $150 million from Russel Wright's American Modern dinnerware service, closed. Pressured by competition from abroad, the industry couldn't adapt fast enough. So now with her children away at school and her husband still in Chicago, Zeisel decided to travel and work abroad. In October 1957 she went to work for Rosenthal in Selb, Germany. Shortly after, in 1958, she visited Mancioli Pottery near

Florence, where she produced some of her favorite tablewares and a series of room dividers based around curvy midriffs with punctuated indents to look like navels.

Zeisel taught for a year at the Rhode Island School of Design in 1960, but her heart was not in it. It was the year her beloved mother died. With little work at home, in 1963 she traveled abroad again, to factories in Japan and India. None of the manufacturing firms put her designs into production. Then in 1964 she undertook what would be her last ceramic design for the next twenty years. At Hyalyn Porcelain in Hickory, North Carolina, she created a series of richly colored glazes and friendly, gently rounded forms, which were ironically reminiscent of objects hand thrown on the wheel.

Zeisel's attentions then turned to the war in Vietnam; she began making antiwar banners, going on peace marches, and undertaking book projects (none of which have ever been published) on subjects ranging from history and politics to childhood and design. "When she stopped designing, she started writing with the same intensity. We listened every day to the newest details she found so exciting," says daughter Jean. "It was laughable in our family that anyone would consider retiring."

The swinging sixties didn't pass fifty-something Eva by. The house in Rockland County was constantly overflowing with young people: former students, friends of her children, and even the odd hitchhiker. Often they came for dinner and ended up staying for six months, hiding out from their unpermissive parents, playing guitar, writing, and generally finding themselves. Eva had only one rule for her young guests: "If there was a pair and they were not married, they had to wake up in different beds. I was very moral," she grins impishly.

The generous supply of young people came in handy when Eva decided to create "a poor woman's palace," extending a garage on her plot to make an additional home. She used salvaged materials from building sites in Manhattan and developed a Rube

Goldberg–like configuration of eccentrically shaped rooms. Needing an electrician, she enlisted a young man who wanted to avoid the Vietnam draft. "He put in innumerable switches, but we don't have much light," she laughs. Over the next seven years, whenever she ran out of money during construction, she simply covered the little house in tarpaulin.

Stephen Rappaport rented Zeisel's little hand-built home in the early 1990s and was so impressed with it that he asked her to design three stores for his Original Leather clothing company in New York. He had no qualms about hiring an octogenarian to design a series of boutiques. "Why not, she is a great designer and the practical response to her work was that my business increased phenomenally," he says. The resulting shop interiors are full of elaborately carved and curlicued wooden shelves that have a primitive folk art appeal. Oddly, Zeisel says her intention was to create a classical look.

In the 1970s Zeisel moved back to Chicago to be with Hans and work on book projects. She restarted her career in ceramic design around 1983 at the time the Musée des Arts Decoratifs de Montréal and the Smithsonian Institution organized a massive retrospective of her work. A major catalyst was a trip to Hungary organized with the help of her younger brother, George. It had been fifty-five years since she had set foot in her homeland. This time she worked at the Zsolnay factory in Pecs, creating elegant statuesque vases and pitchers that shimmer with light reflecting off the exquisite iridescent glazes. Then, in 1985, she designed Pinnacle, a stoneware dinner service for the Japanese company International China.

When Hans died in 1991, Zeisel moved back to New York and immersed herself in her work. "She made one beautiful thing after another," daughter Jean observes. "The way she deals with an unhappy situation is to make beautiful things." Her work is now more diverse than ever before, encompassing everything from bathroom tiles to "closet furniture" (noticing that her young friends were living in ever-smaller apartments, she thought they would benefit from tables, chairs, even shelves that can be folded up and stored in a closet). She found a manufacturer for her midriff-shaped room dividers (they have since popped up in such hip restaurants and hotels as Junno in New York and the Standard in Los Angeles). She also relaunched the Town and Country line and some Schramberg designs in conjunction with the Metropolitan Museum of Art stores.

For her nephew John Striker, president of Brownstone Publishers, she built an elaborate executive office. She didn't wait to get a commission, she simply told him: "Don't buy anything, I will build it all for you." Two months later the furniture arrived—ornamental carved wooden bookcases, a desk, side chairs, two low tables, and four filing cabinets camouflaged as a sideboard. "I would have been the first to say, very nice Eva, and move in a set of lateral files if that had worked better," he confesses. But Zeisel's designs surpassed his rigorous standards. His one worry now is that "stuff keeps going off to museums. I'm waiting for my desk to disappear."

At the start of the twenty-first century, nearly a hundred years since she was born, Eva Zeisel has by her own estimate designed more than 100,000 different objects. She is working at full tilt and is being feted by a growing group of young designers who are just discovering her work and find it is very much of the moment. Maine-based rug designer Angela Adams, with whom she is developing several small rugs, thinks "her bold simplicity could translate into many other mediums."

KleinReid, a young Brooklyn-based duo, have commissioned her to design six vases, a tea set whose lids double as mini-vases, and two tall pitchers. Co-owner James Klein thinks her style is totally in tune with the current mood. "There is a warmth to her work that is refreshing after minimalism without being obviously fussy, coy, or crafty. People need to start understanding the beauty in superfluous curves like hers and not just the usual crappy ceramic forms that are painted up to look like something."

At their first meeting, KleinReid were astonished to find that Zeisel spent six hours discussing ideas. "We started at 8 P.M. and finished at 2 A.M." Her amazing energy is due largely to "chronic projectitis," explains Jean. "She is wildly curious. She will go anywhere at any time of day or night to see anything and she is always very cheerful. If I said let's go to Turkey tomorrow she would up and pack immediately."

Nambé creative director Bob Borden remembers how when she broke her hip in 2002, she continued holding business meetings from her hospital bed. "She is full of octane," he says. "She has this incredible positive core and that translates in the work, which is as passionate as she is."

Eva's mission has always been "the playful search for beauty." For her, design is an act of generosity, not a didactic tool. She never hoped to affect people's lifestyles by her design. She always had more humble ambitions. "I hoped my designs would give pleasure to the user when he had time to notice them, and yet recede when he was too busy or tired."

To Zeisel, the secret of staying constantly at the top of her powers is simply this: "One has to learn not to take oneself too seriously, not to overly respect one's designs. Whatever you aim at and whatever you produce, there are always many more possibilities."

Eva Zeisel,
1935

"SHE IS ABSOLUTELY ONE OF THE GREATS OF TWENTIETH-CENTURY DESIGN," SAYS CHRISTOPHER WILK. "SHE HAS A GREAT LOVE OF PEOPLE AND HOW THEY RELATE TO OBJECTS. HER WORK IS ABOUT THE EMOTIONAL EFFECT THINGS HAVE ON US. IT IS THE MOST ESSENTIAL AND MEANINGFUL ACTIVITY."

Crinkle planters, handmade
and homefired,
c. 1926

Animal dish
for Kispester,
c. 1926

 Teapot, creamer, and teacup
for Schramberg,
1929

 Vases and pitcher
for Schramberg,
1929–30

Inkwell
    for Schramberg,
1929–30

Geometric pieces
    for Schramberg,
1929–30

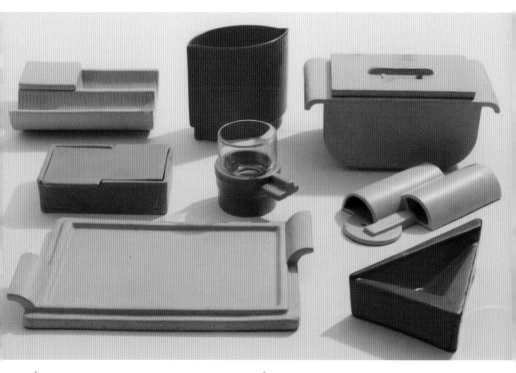

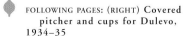
FOLLOWING PAGES: (LEFT) Coffee
    and tea service for Carstens,
1930

FOLLOWING PAGES: (RIGHT) Covered
    pitcher and cups for Dulevo,
1934–35

 Tea set
   for Lomonosov,
1933

Liqueur service
   for Dulevo,
c. 1933–35

PREVIOUS PAGES: (LEFT)
Tea service for Dulevo,
1935

PREVIOUS PAGES: (RIGHT)
Tea service for Dulevo,
c. 1933–35

Prototype for porcelain
Utility Ware,
1942–43

ZEISEL MANAGED TO CRE-
ATE AN IMPRESSIVELY SOPHISTICATED
DESIGN FOR CASTLETON. SHE HAD
READ EMILY POST TO LEARN ALL
ABOUT THE ETIQUETTE OF THE
AMERICAN TABLE AND SHAPED THE
SERVICE TO ILLUSTRATE THE WORDS
"DIGNIFIED," "ERECT," "UPLIFTED."
"I WANTED IT TO LOOK AS IF IT WAS
GROWING UP FROM THE TABLE,"
SHE SAYS. EACH PIECE STARTS OUT
AS STRAIGHT LINES THAT SOFTEN
INTO CURVES. THE WALLS OF EACH
DESIGN ARE THICKEST AT THE
BOTTOM AND TAPER AS THEY RISE.

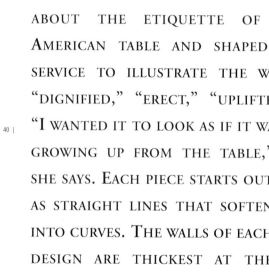

Museum pitcher and coffee cup
for Castleton,
1942–45

Museum bowl with
cover and coffee service
for Castleton,
1942–45

Installation at the Museum
of Modern Art,
1946

ONE OF ZEISEL'S MOST POPULAR DESIGNS IS HER 1946 TOWN AND COUNTRY SERVICE FOR RED WING. THE COMPANY WANTED A DESIGN THAT WOULD BE YOUNG, FREE-SPIRITED, "GREENWICH VILLAGE-Y," AND AFFORDABLE. TOWN AND COUNTRY'S CAPACIOUS, CURVACEOUS, OFF-KILTER SHAPES EPITOMIZE ZEISEL'S PLAYFUL SPIRIT AND ENCAPSULATE HER BELIEF THAT DESIGNS SHOULD COMMUNICATE WITH ONE ANOTHER AND ENGAGE US THROUGH THEIR FRIENDLY, ZOOMORPHIC SHAPES.

◆ *Town and Country* salt-and-pepper
   shakers for Red Wing,
   1946

◆ Eva with
   daughter Jean,
   1942

Town and Country pitcher and
creamer for Red Wing,
1946

Town and Country marmite with
cover, teapot, and sugar bowl
for Red Wing,
1946

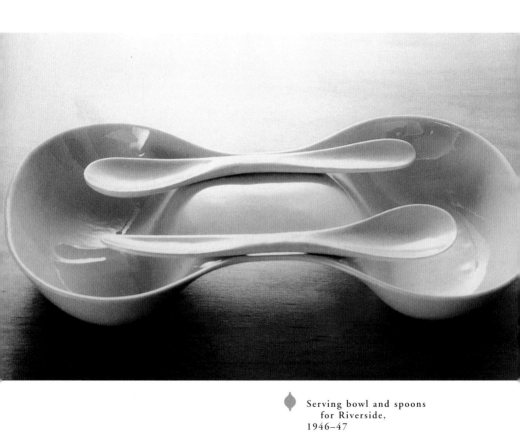

Serving bowl and spoons
for Riverside,
1946–47

Plastic serving dishes
for Cloverware,
1947

Tea service, relish tray, and cruets
for Salisbury Artisans,
1951

Gourd-shaped objects for Hyalyn
Pottery, 1964 and rosewood candle-
stick for Salisbury Artisans,
1951

ANOTHER ONE OF ZEISEL'S MOST CELEBRATED AND SUCCESSFUL DESIGNS WAS HALLCRAFT/ TOMORROW'S CLASSIC. IT VERY NEARLY DIDN'T REACH PRODUCTION. THE MANUFACTURER, HALL CHINA, WAS ON THE POINT OF SHELVING IT WHEN THE PRESIDENT OF COMMERCIAL DECAL STEPPED IN SAYING HE THOUGHT THE PIECES WERE IDEAL FOR DECORATION.

Hallcraft/Tomorrow's Classic
dinnerware for Hall China,
1952

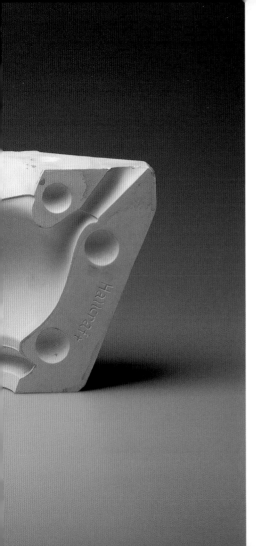

Hallcraft/Tomorrow's Classic mold
and teapots for Hall China,
1952

Hallcraft/Tomorrow's Classic teapot
in Satin Black and Dawn pattern
by Charles Seliger,
1952

SHE BEGINS WITH DRAWINGS AND
PAPER CUTOUTS, THEN SHE CARVES SHAPES TO GIVE THEM A
GREATER FINESSE. "EVERYTHING I DO IS A DIRECT CREATION
OF MY HANDS, WHETHER IT IS MADE IN WOOD, PLASTER, OR
CLAY," SHE SAYS.

◆ Eva with modelmaker at
   Western Stoneware Company,
   1953

◆ Bird-shaped serving pieces for
   Western Stoneware Company, 1953.
   Reproduced with pattern by
   Nikko in 1965.

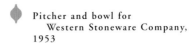

Pitcher and bowl for
    Western Stoneware Company,
1953

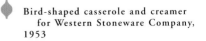

Bird-shaped casserole and creamer
    for Western Stoneware Company,
1953

 Refrigerator jars
for Hall China,
1954

 Teapots for Kispester-Granit
Porcelain Factory,
1983

 Silhouette glassware
for Bryce Brothers,
1952

 Prestige lowball glasses for
the Federal Glass Company,
1954

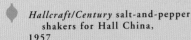

Hallcraft/Century salt-and-pepper
shakers for Hall China,
1957

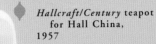

HALL CHINA WAS SO ELATED BY THE
SUCCESS OF TOMORROW'S CLASSIC, IT SOON COMMIS-
SIONED ZEISEL TO CREATE ANOTHER EXQUISITELY REFINED
SERVICE, THE HALLCRAFT/CENTURY LINE. ITS DELICATE
PETAL-SHAPED PLATES RISE UP LIKE THE GRACEFUL ARC OF A
BALLERINA'S ARMS.

FOLLOWING PAGES: *Hallcraft/Century*
pitchers (LEFT) and dinnerware (RIGHT)
for Hall China,
1957

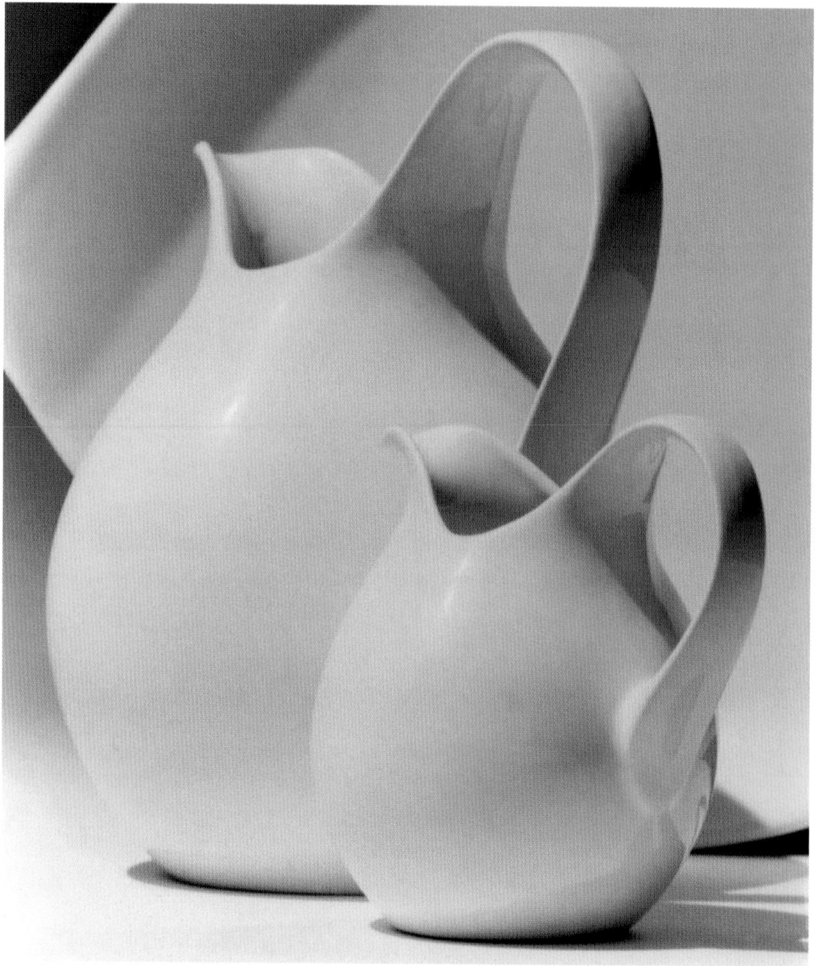

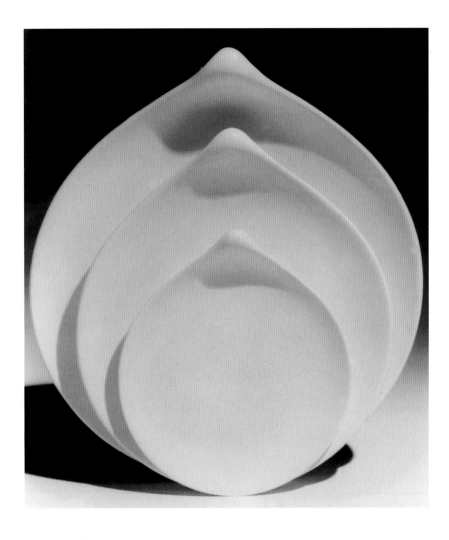

PREVIOUS PAGES:
Hallcraft/Century
dinnerware service
for Hall China,
1957

Eva coffeepot
and sugar bowl
for Rosenthal,
1957–58

Dinnerware
for Mancioli,
1958

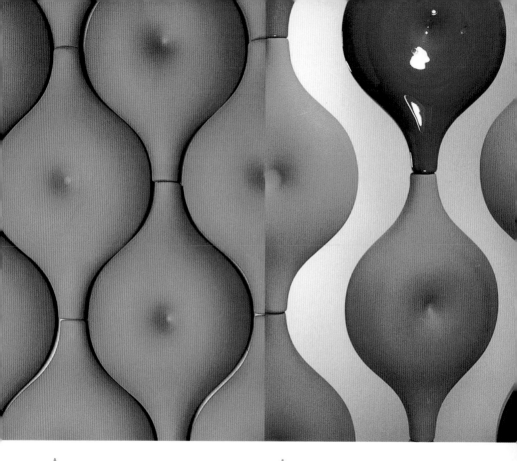

 Belly Button wall divider
for Mancioli,
1958

 The Hollywood Standard Hotel
in Los Angeles,
1999

Patented tubular-steel chairs
shown at the Milan Triennale,
1954

Eva in studio with cutouts,
1997

Ornamental carved
wooden table,
1990s

Carved wooden shelves
for Original Leather store
in New York City, 1997

EVA'S LIFE IS AS EXTRAORDINARY AS HER WORK. SHE DOESN'T FOLLOW TRENDS, DOESN'T BOW TO CONVENTION, AND HAS ALWAYS FOLLOWED HER OWN PATH. DRIVEN BY CURIOSITY AND AN OVERRIDING PASSION FOR NEW EXPERIENCES, SHE CROSSED CONTINENTS TRAVELING ALONE IN AN ERA WHEN WOMEN WERE NOT EXPECTED (OR EVEN PERMITTED) TO GO TO PARTIES WITHOUT A CHAPERONE.

"Eva Zeisel: Designer for Industry" Retrospective Exhibition, 1984

 Stacking bowls
for Kispester-Granit,
1983

 Candlestick, vase, and fruit-shaped
objects for Zsolnay,
1983

Plaster models for *Pinnacle* dinner
service (International China),
1985

Eva working on new designs
with Lomonosov modelmaker
Gyorgi Bugdevich, 2000

 FOLLOWING PAGES: (LEFT) Martini
glass for Bombay Sapphire,
2001

 FOLLOWING PAGES: (RIGHT)
Eva Zeisel vase for Nambé,
2001

Unity accent bowl and platter
for Nambé,
2001

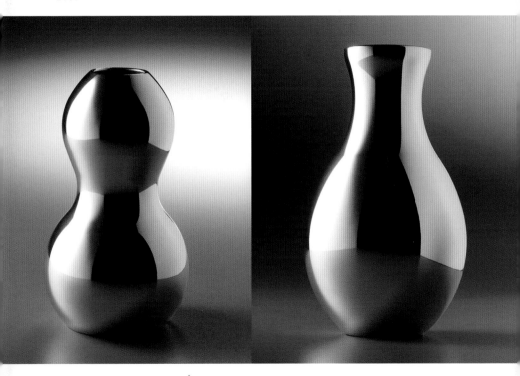

Unity and *Freedom* vases
for Nambé,
2001

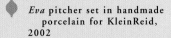

Eva pitcher set in handmade
porcelain for KleinReid,
2002

Eva upright nesting vases in handmade porcelain for KleinReid,
1999

JAMES KLEIN THINKS HER STYLE IS TOTALLY IN TUNE WITH THE CURRENT MOOD. "THERE IS A WARMTH TO HER WORK THAT IS REFRESHING AFTER MINIMALISM, WITHOUT BEING OBVIOUSLY FUSSY, COY, OR CRAFTY. PEOPLE NEED TO START UNDERSTANDING THE BEAUTY IN SUPERFLUOUS CURVES LIKE HERS AND NOT JUST THE USUAL CRAPPY CERAMIC FORMS THAT ARE PAINTED UP TO LOOK LIKE SOMETHING."

FOLLOWING PAGE:
Eva Zeisel,
1999

EVA ZEISEL BIOGRAPHY

1906	Born November 13th in Budapest
1923	Enters the Royal Academy of Fine Arts (Kepzomuveszeti Academia in Budapest)
1924	Becomes the first woman member of the Hungarian Guild of Chimney Sweeps, Oven Makers, Roof Tilers, Well Diggers, and Potters
1925	Visits the Exposition Internationale des Arts Decoratifs et Industriels Modernes in Paris
1927	First job at Hansa Kunstkeramik, a small art pottery studio in Hamburg
1928	Designs over 200 objects for the Schramberger Majolika Fabrik in Schramberg, Germany
1931	Works for Christian Carstens Kommerz Gessellschaft in Germany while living five doors away from the famous Romanisches Café in Berlin
1932	January 1st, visits Russia "to see what is behind the mountain." Designs for the Lomonosov factory near St Petersburg
1934	Works at Dulevo, near Moscow, the world's second largest ceramics factory
1935	Promoted to the post of Artistic Director of the China and Glass Industry in Russia
1936	May 28th, arrested and imprisoned in Moscow on suspicion of plotting to assassinate Stalin
1938	Arrives in Manhattan with $64 in her pocket
1939	Establishes the first American course teaching ceramics as industrial design at Pratt Institute, Brooklyn, New York
1942	Designs America's first Modern, all-white, china dinner service, the Museum line for Castleton China of New Castle, Pennsylvania
1946	The Museum line is presented to the public at a special exhibition at the Museum of Modern Art (Castleton's production was held up due to wartime conditions). Designs the Town and Country service for Red Wing Pottery in Minnesota
1947	Opens a design studio in the basement of her apartment building on Riverside Drive and West 115th Street in New York
1950	Receives a mechanical patent for a tubular steel and canvas chair (now part of the MoMA permanent collection)

EVA ZEISEL BIOGRAPHY (CONTINUED)

1952	Designs Hallcraft/Tomorrow's Classic dinner service for Hall China
1954	Creates the Prestige line for Federal Glass. The glasses are produced at the rate of one a second and sell all over the world
1957	Designs the Hallcraft/Century dinner service for Hall China
1960	Teaches for a year at the Rhode Island School of Design
1963	Creates her last design for 20 years for Hyalyn Pottery, Hickory, North Carolina
1983	Visits the Zsolnay factory in Pecs, Hungary, and designs sculptural modern ceramics using colorful iridescent glazes
1984	"Eva Zeisel: Designer for Industry" retrospective at the Musée des Arts Decoratifs de Montréal, which then travels to America and Europe
1985	Designs Pinnacle dinnerware for International China
1988	Honorary Doctorate from Royal College of Art, London
1991	Honorary Doctorate from Parsons New School, New York City
1995	Designs first of three interiors for the first Original Leather store in New York City
1996	Designs and builds an office interior for John Striker, the president of Brownstone Publishers
1999	Designs line of metal dishes, crystal vases, lamps, and ceramics for Nambé. Creates six Eva vases for KleinReid in Brooklyn, New York. The Metropolitan Museum of Art launches a re-edition of the Red Wing Town and Country line in its stores. "Lost Molds and Found Dinnerware: Discovering Eva Zeisel's Hallcraft," a retrospective of her work at the Schien Joseph International Museum of Ceramic Art, Alfred University, New York. Establishes Eva Zeisel Web site
2000	Returns to Lomonosov in Russia to design a modern tea set. IDSA (Industrial Design Society of America) Bronze Apple Award
2001	Honorary Member, American Ceramics Society. Creates a martini glass for Bombay Sapphire Gin's ad campaign
2002	Receives Pratt Legends Award and Russel Wright Award

INDEX

INDEX (CONTINUED)

PHOTO CREDITS